middle time

Poetry Chapbooks

Melos (Projective Industries, 2015)

The Middle (Omnidawn, 2013)

Second Story of Your Body (Portable Press at Yo-Yo Labs, 2011)

middle time

angela hume

OMNIDAWN PUBLISHING
OAKLAND, CALIFORNIA
2016

Cover art by Mary Burger.
"Optical Occlusions #7" 2015, acrylic on panel, 10 x 12 inches.
www.maryburger.com

Cover and interior typeface: Adobe Electra LT Std

Cover and interior design by Gillian Olivia Blythe Hamel.

Offset printed in the United States
by Edwards Brothers Malloy, Ann Arbor, Michigan
On 55# Heritage Book Cream White Antique

Library of Congress Cataloging-in-Publication Data

Names: Hume, Angela.
Title: Middle time / Angela Hume.
Description: Oakland, California : Omnidawn Publishing, 2016.
Identifiers: LCCN 2015040575 | ISBN 9781632430168 (pbk. : alk. paper)
Classification: LCC PS3608.U438 A6 2016 | DDC 811/.6–dc23
LC record available at http://lccn.loc.gov/2015040575

Published by Omnidawn Publishing, Oakland, California
www.omnidawn.com   (510) 237-5472   (800) 792-4957
10 9 8 7 6 5 4 3 2 1
ISBN: 978-1-63243-016-8

and then the earth
and the world stream's waters vanished into
night

—melic fragment, anonymous

melos

.

(if the life of the mind
  dies with the sun

         who will have seen
      flapping

a sudden
    chirop
      tera

    myo
      desopsia

sequoia
  dendron

shivered
  limb

moon
  a pin   atmospheric

obsidian
  economy of

        river

riprap split
  intimately

like the split down a
       mammal body

    (furious with anyone who

    in the fabrics
  camphor

conifer
  capped

in yellow   (if the sun

were gone
  we wouldn't

know it
              (follow the link to *how hot will it get?*

        threshold beyond
                          which

.

        to go

            the grove
          Santa Lucias

granitic
  basement

batholith to
  bark and cone, fog

        drip
          damp

the fibrous
  bed

(give of the breast
  beneath a head

loam
  timber

(fear
  the war:

dose
  estimation

wrecked
  plant   sievert

.

brain sub
  merged in a bath of heat

and minerals

(sudden epidemi(c
      ology

imagine
  living

two thousand years

(gland
        butterfly-
          shaped

a girl whose cells
  refuse to die

and all the sea

        wells

                    at dusk's farthest edge   river

nowhere
  to go

        light gone out of the sky

rocks and oaks   alders
  blanch

fingers
  reach, the ink

water becomes
  in night

(appearing still   moving

light gone out

         but beyond the
      canopy's blot

sky
  illumes

blue
  in the darkening

.

forest, emaciate
  in the black

bark   bladderlike
       heavier than

air
wa(te)r

elsewhere
　spectral

poison

.

　here　　　　　body's
torsion

sac on the surface
　puncture

(rim fire
　hemorrhage

　here　　　　　my tongue
on your teeth

　in as much of your body as

(possible　　　　earth

capsizing
　toward you

　　　　　unessential
　　　　　world　　　　dissoluble

.

evening moves
　sky-tinted water

(place I'm from

plenty of light
  left   hums

a cut
  clean through

carries
        leaf

tinted
       blue

.

morning's
dehiscence
          melos

Nuttall's
woodpecker

somewhere   (pit*ik*

plumage or oak

(*non-being of each is the other of*
  both

coats

the mind
  watching

      from separate bodies

bright in each, pain
or sugar

we were   *the limit*

is the middle between   *two*

in which
they cease

non-being of
  each   in search of

health
your basic

        beach

egret wisp   brush
  in marsh

takes to flight

(where   does the bird end
                  lagoon begin

geologic fact.   west of
  rift

like all the day's weight
  in sand and

wind   lifting   arid

  reach

back of the
                tongue   a silvering
  globe

lodged like yesterday's
  sex   symptom
so bold

binds like the memory of a first
unkindness

  caved   irreversible
as the palm's chained

       line of the head   which you
trace with her index finger

       (depression   took hold

year of tar
  sands   four-degree

scare
  year of the
aquifer

             at first: night

sweats, night   blight
dreamt of rage's

junk effects   vital functions
  like breathing

and the mind's pigment diffused   a gum
  bichromate

(there, a place for a book on song

the crisis is   the end of the commons   is

very slow
  violence

and we do not heal

    vocalization
declines

in foraging   breeding

  (and we *say*

not because we did not love

.

no longer have we
   desiccates

dinning   lines   the skull's inner
   amplified to such

a pitch

medicate   the withdrawal of
   history

10   then   20   then
   nothing

        stunning
           a warm

   film
   welling   in the stomach

        like a sink   stopped up
   like peace

slept and slept

we were often so

   diffusely
social

.

such small
assemblies

   distributions of
   rescue practice

(number the days
　　the money

involving a question of water   involving

habits of
　　mutual aid

((for four days I remained in the room　　　　　　　　my lungs   arms
　　　　　streaked like a tub　　in my throat
　　copper

voluntary
　　rationing

voluntary
　　association

read:

large volumes of
　　seed
moved from
　　farm to farm, leading to a great
diversity in
　　plants

as in spring　　　on the air　　　odors of
　　skin

rehearse: mutual
　　protection

to make the body more
　　bearable to

regain a *cathexis of the world*

save our life

.

dignity of a Jeffrey
    pine   single

impression
        upon a

bolt of cloth, indigo-dyed   tonight's
  Sierra Nevada

(out from under
  urban land cover

dry day   bedding down   low
  water, bleached

riprap
        crumpled
               skeleton

impossibly
  luminescent—

and you
  what must be

protected

most fiercely: that which
  is past

.

desire
  a search

survivor, in a word: *knife*

or *no*

or a summer of women
spread over the lawn

the list would be endless

the rules of reverence

.

(this collective
  grief noise

no end
  to drought   autumn

  heat

batters bodies
  insides and outsides

dusky
  release of surfaces

deep in the blue
  crescent

between
  tree line and bridge   negative

shaping
  there   opening

you   clutched parts of

me darkly
  inside   and I

didn't stop   no   for once
    followed your body to the center of
mine

.

said: why do we break the social
    body?

said: our bodies have been broken
    into and so we break the social

    body.

.

felt
                    rifting

(incremental
    adaptation

left you with
    visibility

at less than a mile, 80,000
    acres

    I could break
    a tree—

scorched   winds
    high   left you
there

    I could break
    you

now

a new
objective

for a new
world:

   mitigate.
   damage.

.

crustal
    plate

strike-slip   at the transform
                                boundary

all matter moving in one
    direction or

entirely the other

...

think   *flesh without*   *figural unity*
(critical body   functions

think   a tumor bu(r)sts
a loose stitch

...

including   anxiety
          hyper
          activity:

                    (a measure within

normal range

         (girl
           at
         risk

artificial
additives

                  whose
thought to mimic the effects of   estrogen

force the dose   (perfect as an egg

. . .

e.g.,   try
looking away

try looking away try looking away try looking away try looking away try
looking away try

marked by
stuttering   trembling dizziness nausea intrusion of

thoughts

finest pollen   flush   a kind of aka
the season   thisia:

                                           all the windows clapping shut

…

gestational
  BPA
exposure   urine levels   behavioral

      indices
  whose   abstention

     (a girl
      gone
    wrong

second story of your body

—

snowy
plovers

tic in the beach
flesh

tides today at
six-plus feet

a moon at
perigee

(look, irises
open throats

and sea

.

epoxy
resins:

bisphenol A
shatter-

proof
hard and clear

objects
deteriorate

suicides

(Eastern
Garbage
Patch

in the stomachs of fish
plastic

.

write me   field poems

shimizu:

                                            because we
                                            love this place

you want to
see the ocean

that can
be arranged

.

what is the name of the
book on skin

                                            (over and
                                            over

                                            the same
                                            sea, the same

the problem is
the closed system:

nothing at risk of   falling out

.

we say water's
wax-white

like human eyes
after long illness

we say water's
a gorgeous thing

—

risk

there, a brutality

it can't be (any
objectivism

the idea's

a sclerosis

there you go

stoppage

that isn't a car
or a person

a moving that isn't
a moving that isn't

heteronomy

—

what on you
is wrecked

fidelity

(first

(sickness

of contact

(bis
[2-ethylhexyl]

phthalates, found in

some

plastic
food packaging

(sickness

of risk

no sunk
aphorism

*(the house
is gone*

no neatening
wound

(no right life

in the wrong one

—

date of your last
period

         (freak
         exclusion

         a brain's

fork

a torque's
felt.

Where *does*
a poetics

         (first contusion
         experimental

         drag
         purples deep

in a chair no one's
seen

I go to her because
I feel her knowing

We said
it's simple:

what was
now isn't

         here

the woman

—

is there a history of mental
illness in the family   (shrill sero

tonin   low
              horde of bees

orange through
quilt stuff:

see in the   light in the
space   between

                                                             wells of your blood

hundreds of thousands
and counting   (untenable

elsewhere, snow-metal
smell, (woolen) your teeth

there now is a drug
illegible as   the dream

                                                             (your mind

your mind

                                                             is gone

—

eat
against asceticism

a first rendering

a clean meter

fat circulating
in the blood

excess

outside of time

no longer invasive
procedures

help yourself
in(to) time

drainage off
and bleating

you locked clock

1. ...of being borne
2. ...of being upheld

paved or dammed

(be

(the solemn lays

thrush

down its head

a danger

a clean wring

(it's genetic
sympto
matic

into the green

you thin wind
of horse, of spleen

un

bearable
maintainable

for all of time

40

—

refusal's look: an   amen
orrhea

story of body   beveled   years

.

this bay   a finger

this crossing   *breaks*   *the heart*

(like body   gouging
asphalt   e

inter   ruption
pretation

like will to myth
to change

—

one stable bond
one chemic   organo
                                              chlorine

knot, simmer
spate, toxic   loop   loose

in your gut
daughters

                                              (poly
                                              chlorinated
                                              biphenyls

                                              poly
                                              brominated
                                              diphenyl
                                              ethers

                                              phthalates

in ninety-
nine percent

((there was waste
((there was waste

—

immanent   garbage
critique   cut through

precarious
cost

                                            adrift
                                            a binge

affecting

kidneys
the nervous system

                                            (muta
                                            genic

                                            dia
                                            chronic

—

a woman's body   goes out, feigns
                                            reciprocity:

a non-exchange

backward
acts of magic

                                            (once

                                            honed
                                            immanence

—

some release

           (blood coming from her
           nose, her vagina

a person is
systems of trust

(a sill
      on it, a bell

(mean   fact of the disease

—

rifted, we return from the new   hospital:

neat
barbarisms   gone wrong

.

(young jays
ransack the understory

.

pending trial

whose   testimony
whose   scrap of democracy

(today a woman's body   eats itself

—

in   operable

begin   to begin to   fray

outside, the social   thickening
(when were we younger

—

strict embolisms   detonate
the noon

(enter   said cave of losses

nutrients
blast open a vein

.

and the slick   takes
to the glade

(*fuels, will continue*   *to fuel*

and the pain is   excruciating—

nothing any good

—

body occurs at   a limit

a tissue
limit

a blood
limit   (2-

a broken-cell   (butoxy
                                            (ethanol

limit

what kind of limit   are you

.

wear air-
supplied breathing

          apparatuses to   protect your
                                            nose

                                            throat
                                            and lungs

wear nitrile or PVC
gloves and

chemical-splash
goggles to   protect your
                                            skin and eyes

(say: an art
blackens as a river

in sickness
                    bends

in the case of
exposure
                                                        call

.

whose
other   are you

                                      (*the measure of the
                                      actual body / is*

                                      the measure

trick
zero

sub
cutaneous

limit

garbage-
cell

limit

(the limit
is said

.

what kind of song   if you'll sing

((what kind of song
will you sing   if you'll sing

.

if:

body's
impenetrable

if:

body begins and ends
against

                                                     body
no longer   exists

—

toxins, unextraordinary
bang out days

(neoplasia—
in fact

a second skull

.

the child's gone   we thought years

with which to
fuck the sick

environmental hazards

(utter
ordination

nightmares

between the legs

body
with body to give

this time
away

—

touched but

(a head
pouring out

(some) story wastes
into myth—

(terrible as it is, it is
a half-life, calculable

horror, eventual
blisters of light

reeking, bold as only
the wealthy

(if it had been yours,

we say, imagine

the waste

from the train
bay, blister, or steel

history, whelm
the myth

—

lacking
        measure   (*in her*

incredible need

                                         separation

fell
the dwelling

(toward a sojourn   that isn't
evisceration

.

know:

the network is sick
when you   cut out of

the woman
a lone   methodology

Antigone
                        's *thrēnos*

                                       (a)por(i)ous

.

were it not for the
orders of music   *hidden / we should be*

claimd by the pre
ponderant void

                                    first:

there was

                                    humming—

...

a violence   white, a sink of milk
(predicative of

                                              chlorpyrifos
                                              containers for brutal acts

long-term   population-level
impacts

...

      (sub-   lethal bio   logical
      effects (write

repugnant
that is,   body scuds
      across the brown

...

binding   act
  secret   ion

bio
  accumu
lation

(over *virtually all the earth*

(consider the case of maize

For in the exercise of violence over life and death more than in any other legal act, law reaffirms itself. But in this very violence something rotten in law is revealed.

—Walter Benjamin

fragments

.

habitat loss

water   air   ultra
violet

light

radiative
sub-

cut
  aneous

light

we are

forcing
names

.

first
   demarcate

an aesthetics of
   injury

.

((touch me there
   please

.

first
   ask a name for

this disease

.

the truth that nature
   means in me

．

((grown thick, thick
 with we

no one ever touches us   …   create no value

.

blunt
objects   bone   fracture

                    speech centers   leave torn
             human breasts, cleave
                  skulls

(("non-lethal"   rubber wax plastic wood   projectiles

                    loathe the body, own
                          the hema
                       toma

the object's: pain

.

war
on

health

slow sinning, smacks of

(task: locate some evicted
  cut

(inhabit that   wealth
  incision

in such a way that can't be used

.

state of pacifi
cation state of

damage state
of destroy all
ex

cess   body
state of little
to no

speech

ill
state

police
state

.

noonish moan, slight
as a relic

(somebody
botched the lawn

we want:
immunity

(that is,
ceremony

exception to
exception

(what we want is

.

no, riot
nothing

holy
(frenzied

clutch   the land
still

born
(coordinated

administered
harm

(cultivate
                                              sanctuary

...

toxic   tri
   panic   clos
                         an

                         at
              ra
                         zine

are we feminizing our baby boys?

assault on the male: our future at risk

first, a series of
   glands

[combining] elements of two or more animal
   forms

a smear
   in the bile   the milk

  .

fear
   the girl

(initially absorbed through
   tissue in the mouth

hard palate   soft
   upper and lower
teeth

site of   threat displays   panting   production of
  sounds

repulsively

into the
  child

creature
  large, ugly, and frightening

the downward tilt of
  any glans

.

incomplete
  masculinization

(providing excellent control over
  how much chemical gets into the
mouse

something about how
  sperm is made

of a
  degree

incompatible

(*pass down to your children grandchildren and great-grandchildren your blue eyes*
  left-handedness

not a lifetime of
  toxic exposures

fix it.
so kids can be normal

Now a whole is that which has beginning, middle, and end. A beginning is that which is not itself necessarily after anything else, and which has naturally something else after it; an end is that which is naturally after something itself, either as its necessary or usual consequent, and with nothing else after it; and a middle, that which is by nature after one thing and has also another after it.

—Aristotle

the middle

May launches
a rig   drags

wood, shrub
another   purpler

middle term

another clearer
sediment, perigee

moon, over
grown

would you have
wanted your life

to rain   thrash   the drowned
nest

found   woman

spruce out back

would you have
taken it   down

snarled in a wire
meant you were twelve

there   sealed
her own

jug   triang
  ular

there   a middle
stroke

do you experience

depression   embarrassment   painful

intercourse   hair   a lining

knit of teeth

(spread
  the pack   bring

(water

regret   a dearth
bores   a drill

only after
a symptom

                                              makes of
                                              your body

a middle

or cave   a derelict

quiet   the spigot

                    sealed off

casked away   as any oath
a blasphemy

                    profound
                    boredom

on its reel
spinning out

I will (fidelity) but
don't know how to

protect   oneself

                    one body
        means nothing to anything

captive   cry (ology

                    pressed as
                middle time:

the temporality
of the middle is

              the temporality of waste

an aesthetics of the middle
dreams in skin   for years

I wasted my body
tight   coil round a hook

without
consequence   the planet

dimming like any
one

encysted, time
spent in such a way

we did not have to   reckon with it

force the middle its

non-ache   ultradian
cycling

                                                most earthly

condition

for those who
know no earth

in the drift   the middle's
difficulty

                                  wood thrush
point-seven parts   per million

busted birth   nest
                    left

neuro
toxins

and so on
through the food chain

rusty blackbird's
forest   litter   second
                               profanation

never a question of
whether   *(also another after*

song   awaiting
                     vocalization

                       awaiting
                   a present

                      a waiting
                far from whole

time of sheet   melt
time of cicadas

there was love and then
there wasn't

                                                    (stone
                                    hill stone   fruit

time of panic   buy
time of food   riots

there was
sickness like

a pregnancy and then   there wasn't

                                    (animal or a god

watching cold   as though
from another room

                                    whose name is
                                        Precarity

one might say: hottest on record

one might say: faster than models can
                                                capture

one might say: persistence of desire

one might say:

1700 miles of   energy security
                              crosses hundreds of bodies

bit   open fluid pockets
   umen

viscous   omen   (won't flow unless heated
found   diluted

leaking
   crude:

work of the middle   (surfactant

metal hollow (ed-out
foul (ing   air   water   land

                                                  once

water
f(ol)lowed

when the oil when   the food when
we are well again   will we conceive

a child   crystalline
structures

set to generous   music

       (difficult as stopping a
love

from devouring a   sharded
mind

firm   diagnosis

white atmosphere
sick now with snow

        awaiting
        burial

ask: one in three? one
in five? would you

have done what we did?

when the water
runs out the middle

runs out   until then

iron river   ripped   darker

in this summer of   morning

carbon
sink   conifers   combing out the light

road and mill
pulp stink   film

a tongue
scum   somnolent

inside of a house, basically
chlorides, urine   pulse

                  (100000 square kilometers a day
                      fighting back

ordinary hour
          tracing   now

now   now

goes and
goes

notes

Some of the language in this book is adapted from published reports on health and environmental research findings, including reports published by/ at the EPA, Louisiana State University, *Pediatrics*, www.extinctioncrisis.org, the IPCC, and many others.

—

melos

Some of the fragments in this series echo Mei-mei Berssenbrugge, Brenda Hillman, and Lorine Niedecker.

The epigraph is from *Greek Lyric Poetry*, translated by M.L. West.

Page 9: *if the life of the mind / dies with the sun* references "Can Thought go on without a Body?" in *The Inhuman: Reflections on Time*, by Jean-Francois Lyotard.

Pages 14-15: The italicized text is from Hegel's *Science of Logic*.

Pages 18-19: Some of the language in these fragments is from or resembles language from *The Withdrawal of Tradition Past a Surpassing Disaster* by Jalal Toufic and *Thinking in an Emergency* by Elaine Scarry.

Pages 20-22: Some of these fragments are for a handful of fearless women, trans, and non-binary poets in the Bay Area, with love.

Page 21: In Anne Carson's translation, Elektra cries, "Oh my friends, / in times like these, / self-control has no meaning. / Rules of reverence do not apply" (see *An Oresteia*).

Page 22: *I could break a tree— / I could break you* is from H.D.'s poem "Garden" in *Sea Garden*.

—

Page 27: The italicized text is from Adriana Cavarero's book *Horrorism: Naming Contemporary Violence*.

—

second story of your body

This series is for G.N., G.H., and R.L.

Pages 33-35: These fragments are for the Point Reyes Station "Geography of Hope: Reflections on Water" community (March 18-20, 2011), whose words, reflections, and knowledges inspired, and on occasion found their way into, these fragments.

Page 33: *objects / deteriorate / suicides* gestures toward Alfred North Whitehead's claim in *Science and the Modern World* that "any physical object which by its influence deteriorates its environment, commits suicide."

Page 34: *over and over, the same sea, the same* is adapted from Elizabeth Bishop's poem "At the Fishhouses."

Page 37: The italicized text points toward aphorisms 18, 20, and 29 of Theodor W. Adorno's *Minima Moralia*.

Page 40: The italicized text is from Germaine Knoblauch Norris's unpublished poem "Evening."

Page 41: The italicized text is from Jean-Luc Nancy's piece "Shattered Love," which appears in *The Inoperative Community*.

Page 49: The first line of this fragment echoes Jean-Luc Nancy in his piece "Corpus." Nancy writes, *"Bodies don't take place in discourse or in matter...* They take place at the limit, *qua limit...*the fracture and intersection of anything foreign in a continuum of sense, a continuum of matter."

Page 50: *the measure of the actual body / is the measure* is from section 4 of Michael Palmer's poem "The Leonardo Improvisations," which appears in *At Passages*.

Page 51: The italicized text is from Jean-Luc Nancy's piece "Fifty-eight Indices On the Body."

Page 54: *in her incredible need* is from section 32 of George Oppen's poem "Of Being Numerous."

In Greek tragedy, the staged lamentation of the chorus and of certain women figures is called *threnos*. It was considered contrary to political discourse. But as Nicole Loraux points out in her book *The Mourning Voice: An Essay on Greek Tragedy*, such tragic figures as Cassandra and Antigone appropriated lamentation for their own purposes, inflecting it with a politics—as Loraux terms it, an "anti-political" politics of the feminine. And while *threnos* was considered incompatible with lyric, in tragedy *threnos* became associated with song, a form of lyre-less music. Through this song without lyre, Loraux argues, spectators were moved to think beyond their citizen status and toward their more essential relation to all the living.

were it not for the orders of music hidden / we should be claimd by the preponderant void is from Robert Duncan's poem "Four Pictures of the Real Universe," which appears in *The Opening of the Field*.

Page 55: In her essay "On Song, Lyric, and Strings," Brenda Hillman writes, "Whether song came before speech, we just don't know. No one can tell from fossil jawbones whether the first sounds were humming or grunting." This last fragment is after B.H.

—

fragments

The epigraph is from Walter Benjamin's essay "Critique of Violence."

Page 64: The italicized text is from the section of Robert Duncan's *Dante Études* entitled "On Obedience."

Page 65: The italicized text is from the French collective Tiqqun's *Introduction to Civil War*.

Pages 66-69: These fragments were written after the October and November 2011 acts of police violence against protestors in Oakland, Berkeley, and Davis, California.

—

Pages 71: Some of this language is from features at Fox News (Deirdre Imus, "Green Your World") and Public Radio International (Ashley Ahearn, "Living on Earth"). These pages reflect on the critical work of Giovanna Di Chiro, who argues that anti-toxics discourse risks reproducing heterosexist, queerphobic, and eugenics logics. See her article "Polluted Politics? Confronting Toxic Discourse, Sex Panic, and Eco-Normativity" in *Queer Ecologies: Sex, Nature, Politics, Desire*.

—

the middle

The epigraph is from Aristotle's *Poetics*.

Page 77: Language here echoes that of both Virginia Woolf (in *To the Lighthouse*) and Rachel Blau DuPlessis. With reference to Doris Lessing's story "Dialogue," DuPlessis writes, "The female mode of seeing…a constellated integrative form. This vision contains feminine, transcends masculine, asserts female as synthesis…This structure is parallel to the double status of Mrs. Ramsay in Lily's painting…that stroke in the middle, the one unifying lighthouse stroke, which is love and ambition, mother and child, death and pleasure: the female synthesis" (see "For the Etruscans" in *The Pink Guitar: Writing as Feminist Practice*).

Page 79: This fragment contains traces of Giorgio Agamben on oath (see his book *The Sacrament of Language*).

Page 84: The lines *would you / have done what we did?* echo Sylvia Plath's "The Hanging Man."

acknowledgments

Thank you to the following editors and publications, in which versions of some of the fragments in this book appear: Hugh Behm-Steinberg, *Eleven Eleven*; Marthe Reed (guest ed.), *Dusie Magazine*; Brian Ang, *Armed Cell*; Jimmy Lo (guest ed.), *Little Red Leaves*; Lily Brown and Claire Becker, *RealPoetik*; Roland Pease, *Zoland Poetry*; Jared Schickling, *eccolinguistics*; Jonathan Minton, *Word for/ Word*; Adam Peterson (guest ed.), *NOÖ*; and C.E. Harrison, *Spinning Jenny*.

Thank you to Brenda Iijima of Portable Press at Yo-Yo Labs for publishing "second story of your body" as a chapbook; to the Omnidawn editors and the 2012 Omnidawn Chapbook Prize judge Joseph Lease for choosing to publish some of the fragments in this book along with "the middle" as a chapbook; and to Stephanie Anderson, Karen Lepri, and Kate McIntyre of Projective Industries for publishing "melos" as a chapbook.

Sincere thanks to those who thought with me about aspects of this book at its various stages: Brenda Hillman, Rusty Morrison, Gillian Osborne, Evelyn Reilly, Frances Richard, Mary Wilson, Laura Woltag, and especially Gillian Hamel. Thank you to Joe Lewandowski for always believing in my work. Thank you again to Mary for helping me to see this book through, and for the most generous love. Thank you, finally, to my family for endless encouragement.

Angela Hume is the author of the poetry chapbooks *Melos* (Projective Industries, 2015), *The Middle* (Omnidawn, 2013) and *Second Story of Your Body* (Portable Press at Yo-Yo Labs, 2011). Individual poems have appeared in *Eleven Eleven, Dusie Magazine, Armed Cell, Little Red Leaves, RealPoetik, eccolinguistics, Zoland Poetry, Spinning Jenny, The Portland Review*, and elsewhere.

Middle Time by Anglea Hume

Cover art by Mary Burger.
"Optical Occlusions #7" 2015, acrylic on panel, 10 x 12 inches.
www.maryburger.com

Cover and interior text set in Electra LT Std

Cover and interior design by Gillian Olivia Blythe Hamel.

Offset printed in the United States
by Edwards Brothers Malloy, Ann Arbor, Michigan
On 55# Heritage Book Cream White Antique

Omnidawn Publishing
Richmond, California
2016

Rusty Morrison & Ken Keegan, senior editors & co-publishers
Gillian Olivia Blythe Hamel, managing editor
Melissa Burke, marketing manager
Cassandra Smith, poetry editor & book designer
Peter Burghardt, poetry editor & book designer
Sharon Zetter, poetry editor, book designer & development officer
Liza Flum, poetry editor & marketing assistant
Juliana Paslay, fiction editor
Gail Aronson, fiction editor
RJ Ingram, *OmniVerse* contributing editor
Kevin Peters, marketing assistant & *OmniVerse* Lit Scene editor
Trisha Peck, marketing assistant
Sara Burant, administrative assistant
Josie Gallup, publicity assistant
SD Sumner, publicity assistant

Publication of this book was made possible in part by gifts from:
Robin & Curt Caton
John Gravendyk